As It Is In Heaven . . .

As It Is
In
Heaven . . .

Selected poems of
Jock McKeen

with commentary by
Bennet Wong

PD Publishing

© 1993 J. McKeen and B. Wong. All rights reserved

PD Publishing
Haven By-the-Sea
Site 9 - Davis Road
Gabriola Island, British Columbia, Canada V0R 1X0

Canadian Cataloguing in Publication Data

McKeen, Jock, 1946–
    As it is in heaven

    Poems.
    I. Wong, Bennet, 1930–   II. Title.
PS8575.K43A88 1993   C811'.54   C93-091487-2
PR9199.3.M235A88 1993

    ISBN 0-9696755-1-X

Published under the auspices of the *Journal of Child and Youth Care*.

Printed and bound in Canada by Hignell Printing Limited

∞ This book is printed on acid-free paper.

Contents

Illustrations

AS IT IS IN HEAVEN . . .

This is the odyssey of one man with whom I have shared some twenty creative and exciting years.

During the process of discovering the comforts and terrors of a life together, Jock has chronicled his inner experiences through the writing of his poetry.

As is the case with the endless myriad of sensitive, lonely boys everywhere, fearful of the cruel rejection and taunts of peers, Jock secreted his poetic and musical nature behind a series of conforming masks and defenses. He found *inner* solace and consolation behind the closed doors of his bedroom while forging an *outer* life of acceptance through scholarship and achievement.

Upon first meeting Jock, *the man*, it was this hidden, vulnerable boy who first touched my heart. I laughed at the carefully groomed macho manikin that he presented with the confidence of a salesman who had experienced a lifetime of impressing others with his looks and manner. That laugh shook his world and frightened his sensitive inner boy. Yet, it was that very recognition that stimulated his curiosity and steered him into the crosscurrents of the rapids that was to become our relationship.

For years, Jock would journal his experiences in his poetry in isolation, fearful even of my critical gaze. Only after years of testing was he able to tentatively show me what he had been writing. To his amazement, I did not laugh. On the contrary, I was moved to tears; the words revealed the soul of the hidden boy.

Jock, *the boy*, has borne the responsibility of preserving the tender *yin* nature of Jock's being. These treasures have been carefully hidden; only when I had passed the most rigorous of tests were they shyly shown to me in a most tentative act of faith.

To my astonishment, Jock's lines sang to me the music of the spheres, reflecting the revelations of our relationship. They *embodied* what we were discovering — that whatever it was that we were identifying as spiritual, what many refer to as "God" was being revealed in the nature of our relationship. Individually, each of us was discovering the autonomous pattern of ourselves in our bodies, our minds, our emotions and our spiritual natures through being revealed *in relationship*.

In expressing *himself* in his poetry, Jock has expressed *ourselves*, and vice versa. Isomorphically, the revelation of the self, the other, the relationship with others and with nature are all the stuff of the order of the universe. As is reminiscent in the song from the play, "Les Misérables":

"To love another person is to see the face of God."

These first poems are the revelations of my friend whose words seem to know the face of God.

Ben

Gestation

I am pregnant — and the birth seems imminent

Poems have been gestating — for years

I feel the dense feelings stirring
and the slight nausea of the inward sea-change

Waiting still
I pray for the poems to rise to birth in me

Now I begin to see
how to harvest what I have been incubating

Permit a mood to overwhelm
feel the interior vertigo
yet stay standing

The inner wind begins to blow
images swirl like dry leaves
in circles

Don't try to catch them
pick up the ones that
come to light

And assemble them at your writing table

SO IT IS IN NATURE

Jock's fondest boyhood memories centre around his summer vacations in the woods of northern Ontario. The colours and sounds, that stimulated a host of Canadian artists, burned into his blood, forever influencing his appreciation of music, art and nature.

Especially important to him in those halcyon days was the experience of fishing with his favorite uncle whose tenderness and caring inspired and supported Jock's own sensitive nature.

It was during one of our own summers of fishing on the sea with our three sons that Jock dragged a large stingray to the water's surface. Appearing like an alien otherworldly creature with large, soulful eyes that seemed to speak to its captors, this creature from the deep stimulated a spiritual awareness that Jock was moved to memorialize in "Denizen Eyes."

As a boy, Jock loved flowers; however, to admit to this would have provoked much teasing and rejection from his peers. Consequently, he refused to have any kind of relationship with plants other than at a distance. When Jock, *the man*, began to help me with the garden, all flowers were identified as "zinnias." Only later did he allow his

6

passion for plants and gardens to flourish without shame. His most creative interest proved to be in the art of raising and sculpting bonsai plants, a family of which he continues to tend.

At the same time, Jock began to write about the beauty he found in sunsets, in forests, in the oceans and all around him. Many times I have watched him whistling bird songs to caged birds that sing to him appropriate, although somewhat puzzled, responses, as he describes in "Duet." In "Windows," he writes about the time that a hummingbird was able to settle into his hand in order to be carried out of doors, instead of injuring itself against a window.

As a child, Jock took piano lessons which he loved; but many a time he was beaten up by neighborhood bullies who labelled him a "sissy." He, himself, would then dismiss musicals and opera as being frivolous or symptomatic of the effeminate. Through his adolescent years, much of his inner nature was repressed.

Now, he can wear pink with pleasure, and feel the headiness in the stimulation of all of his senses. Music seems to pour from his veins through a great variety of instruments such as the piano, saxophone, clarinet and flute. He thrills to a broad range of musical expression, from rock to classical, and can even sing with utter abandon.

Now, he is shamelessly ecstatic over a bird's song, the hues of a sunset, the colours and scents of flowers, the taste of honey. Gaining his confidence in himself has been rewarded with his reclaiming his sense of delight.

Ultimately, his appreciation of *grace* and *beauty* finds expression in his pen, as witnessed in the following group of his poems.

Ben

Denizen Eyes

I. Boyhood

As a boy
*   I would stalk fish*
spending hours rowing over watery terrain:
*   lily pads, muck, misty mornings*
*   rainy afternoons, sunny lonely days*
in pursuit

The spirituality
*   of the aloneness*
*   crept up on me*

A boy with nature:
I responded like a lover
*   to the winds*
*   the clouds*
*   the sun*
*   the rain*
the moods of the water
the trees by the rocky shore

I learned to read beneath the surfaces
*   to imagine holes, caverns, grottoes*
*   where the lunkers would lie*
I trolled for muskellunge
*   a fresh water Leviathan*

I even caught one, undersized
*   and hooked one more*
I remember the disdainful, hateful look
*   as that muskie rose to the surface*
*   to shake himself free from*
*   my paltry effort*

I didn't know then
*   that all the while I was trolling*
Something was trolling for me:
In my pursuit, I was hooked
*   by the God of the Wind*

I learned to find fish
  see what they would want
read water
  imagine what lay beneath
Success in the catch:
  pride and manhood in the bent rod

When my childhood hero died
  I was suddenly, harshly, adult
the death of former dreams
  and the birth of my personal promise

I then fished utterly alone
  and went on to other things
Still, at times, I would remember
  the pull on the pole
as I felt a big one fight me back

II. Ocean

Years later:
  Desolation Sound
    ocean now
I was beginning to face depth
  in relationship
I began to fish again
  not trolling now
    mooching
  for bottom fish
    300 feet down
in the deep hole we were shown
  by the old fisherman

At the changing of the tide —
  Wham!
fish after gigantic fish

A resurgence:
  we fished often
    under a vast open sky

mostly to enjoy the eternity of the landscape
   a stretch of gleaming water
   mountains all around
   aloneness
at the edge of the universe

We saw whales breach
   one swam under the boat
heard loons crying
   in the morning mists
We caught red snappers
   orange bloated creatures
that were torn from the depths
   and could not go back down

I was stalking again . . .

III. The Visit

One day — the tug on the rod
   was so intense
I was angry with my son — I though he had
caught bottom
   in irritation, I took the rod
     thinking to coax the hook away from
      a submerged log or tire
pulling with my whole body weight
   the rod tip dipped under the water
     as if to pull us all down
if I heaved hard enough
   either we would be pulled to the bottom
or the bottom of the sea would have to come to us
   narrowing the barrier of water that lies between
     closing the gap that intervenes
And imperceptibly — a yielding!
Straining, I leaned with full weight
   to raise the piece of bottom
     probably an old log that had
      lain for years
   dead solid weight
   pulling again and again
     sweat and sinewy torment

A Herculean labour
I began to gain

Peering down
* into the green shadowy depth*
* watching for the lunker to come up*
I saw
* an immense cloud*
*   of darkness*
rising

A shape began to appear
* looming huge in the gloomy shadows*
where the light did not penetrate

Then in the final pull, it floated up
* like some dark spectre from another world*

Large wings
I caught a glimpse of the barbed tail
Fear shuddered through me
We had hooked a ray — and it could not get free
If I pulled it into the boat, we could be injured
It was hooked solidly — through one wing

A creature of darkness
* bottom consciousness*
from another zone
* rising up*
erupting into the light of day

I was not prepared
* for the electric shock*
that went through me
* as I saw the face*
a pleading, toothy mouth underneath
* and strange bronze, golden-rayed eyes*
studying me

I wanted to set it free
But how? To bring it into the boat
* would be disaster*

In the moment, I began to talk
    quietly, as a friend
telling it I wanted to have it go free
    but I needed to release the barb
I made a bargain — be still and I will
    hurt you as little as possible

The golden-rayed eyes viewed me
    trustingly

I seized one fin with rusty pliers,
    expecting a tumult to erupt

Instead, the eyes continued to watch
    silently, placidly
    with deep creature emotion filling them
I believe the beast was in pain
    yet it surrendered to my
    quiet voice, and fumbling attempt

After much effort — the hook released
    and I watched it float free

Again — I expected a violent splash
    to assure freedom

Instead, it seemed to have read my intent
    because it lingered
lolled in the bright water, just beneath the surface
    and rolled over to look me deep into my eyes

Sending a mystical communion of eye beams
    before it gracefully turned and
        began to fly
          down
        into the depths
slowly passing beyond human view
    into the green shadows

and disappeared

leaving me weeping
    with the impact of
        the meeting

IV. Rebirth

new cleansed feeling
  like the freshness after a summer rain
    the atmosphere new

and a closeness with the boys
  who had witnessed the event with me

Since meeting this representative of
  bottom consciousness
I have not had the heart
  to fish again

And yet
  in setting the creature free
I have been hooked
  caught into a whirlwind
    of my own craving
      for surrender

The creature of the bottom
  is tugging at me

I must now make
  my own
    deep voyage

Boyhood Images

I play again
  with the wooden toys
of my youth:
  awakening the sensuality
of my boyhood
  joined with nature

I run barelegged
  on mossy rocks
and smell the breezes
  flowing through young trees

I feel the harsh
  razor pain of
a clamshell cut
  on a tender foot
and watch the salty
  red blood flow

I drink fresh
  spring water
with the sweet metallic taste
  of the tin dipper

I live in solitariness
  sitting
on a rough board
  feet dangling in the water
feeling the sun
  bake my shoulders
and watch the brilliant
  purple dragon fly

I walk barefoot at night
  on damp grass
the whippoorwill chants
  in the fragrant darkness

14

I feel morning dew beneath my bare feet
    soft grass blades between my toes
then walk on wet brown sand
    and feel the sudden awakening
as my steps enter the cold water

I hear the creaking of my oars
    in the morning mist
the rough grooved handles
    feel cold in my hands
the water makes a lush patter
    as it drips from the returning blades
my pants are wet from the damp boat seat

My fishing rod bobs its rhythmic pulse
        tug   tug   tug
the line trolling far behind the boat

Lily pads gently scrape the boat's side
I hear a splash in the distance
    and up close the insistent buzz of a bee
the pungent smell of the water lilies permeates me

I face the dark forest
    that stretches for miles
then penetrate it, become familiar
    with dark, sweet green

The air hangs still
    on a hot summer afternoon
I stand high on the rock face
    and witness the water below
        peering in from the sky
to look beneath the surface
    to see what God sees
I dream
    with clean air
in my boy lungs

Green Song

Climbing the stair
  I suddenly encounter
the little bonsai tree
  celebrating spring

  the whole trunk is arched
in riotous mirth
  new wild growth
spraying from its proud branches
  thrusting skyward in exaltation

a green-leafed gloria

confident
  alive
thrilling
  with the sapsurge
    of renewed life

little tree,
  if you had a face
you would be
  grinning wildly

if you had eyes
  they would be
sparkling and illuminated

you are
  singing your heartwood
emanating an aura of health and vitality

laughing in lush
  green-leafed splendour

you stretch
    ecstatically
throwing back your branches
    in abandon
delirious
    with the sensuous delight
of wind, rain
    and warming sun

and here,
    at evening
you are
    voicelessly
singing

a solitary hymn
    of joy

Sunset

On calm summer evenings
  we gather, looking westward
to watch the sun
  go down over the water and mountains
with music and camaraderie

Often
  after the brilliant glory has sunk
    and the cool night air descends,
we stand together, basking
  in the warmth of our closeness
and watch the changes
  as the light's intensity fades

Sometimes, in the afterglow
  a special locus opens:

  a pink colour rises
from the horizon
and suddenly, seamlessly
    leaps
to the billowy clouds in the
  immense blue sky overhead

the sky is so huge
  it hurts to look
yet, we strain to see
  as colour flows east
    above us

the light spreads
  its pink wonder
across the open sky
  dancing from cloud to cloud
  colouring the whisps
like cotton candy

we arch back,
  into awkward positions
    to follow the colour's liquid movement,
straining to see the vault
  softly ignited

Our spines strain
to look back and up;
  the world is upside down
and gloriously coloured
  the ground is replaced by a carpet of
blue sky with suspended coloured clouds

as we struggle,
our bodies are bent
  into new configurations

  vision snaps
into a new angle
and we see with new eyes:
  our reborn perspective
throws the world into movement

  suddenly we are
tumbling together,
  cartwheeling backwards;

in this shared tilted vision,
the sky inside opens
  and we are flooded
with the glory
  of awesome peace
and profound satisfaction

then, in a blink
  the pink is gone
we stand upright once more
  under the darkening sky

swallows dart and wheel
  over our heads
cavorting in the twilight air

and the afterglow
    echoes
in the clouds
    of our reborn souls

Duet

(Sek Kong, November 1989)

We strolled in the street
    of the Chinese village
where I met
    the caged grey bird
warbling with full responsiveness
    reaching through the bars
across the chasm

Hearing my whistle,
    he cocked his head
studying me
    then blazed into open-mouthed song
sending a gloria resounding
    across the dusty street

The villagers grinned at the spectacle
    of a silly white man
whistling to a little bird

I was captivated,
    my focus narrowed
the world opened
    and we were alone together

Peering into his open beak
    I saw the vibrating tongue
and deeper
    into the cavern
        of silence
where all songs originate

Becoming inventive,
   I would fashion new whistles
and the little bird
   joined with me
delighting in his copied response

Song within silence
   birthed
a subtle movement
   of darkness and light

As his melody soared,
   a flame ignited
then flared
   into brilliance
illuminating
   this magic locus

In the crystalline purity
   of the moment
our songs danced
   together
over the light beams

When he could not match,
   his vitality dimmed
his whole body sank
   into a dejected, lost
pose of futility

a cloud of darkness enveloped
   his little presence
and the air was heavy
   with death

Then, wondrous resurrection:
   the spark reappeared in his eyes
he would rise earnestly
   to study me
      and try once more

he puffed his body
and burst forth
into song
dispersing the dark mist
light dawned again

At times, he arched back
opened his throat full
and trilled with his whole body
in ecstatic pleasure
thrilling to be addressed
beast and human in song

The sweet purity
of the caged bird
ready to give
full throat
to a new song
set chords playing in me

In the cage, he is free
outside, we are slaves
to so many conventions
that squash responsiveness

I have been returned
to the Garden,
fed by the
freewheeling joy
and bounty
of his celebration

He has liberated me
with his dedication

Now,
my own soul
begins to sing
an ancient
song of praise

Windows

I. Barrier

An invisible barrier
   separates
the human world
   and the magic of
nature

In our little lives,
   we are trapped
      within
   civilized encumbrances,
      isolated
We can look out
but transparent panels
   separate
      us from
the life that could be:
   full-blooded
   soul and heart alive
   relishing breezes, smells, tastes
      out in the clearing
   feeling a sun full
      on exposed skin
   relating to other creatures

At quiet times
   distant songs hint
at vitality beyond
   the death of
the moment

My life too is like this
   I can see
      pictures
   even clearly
      sometimes

but
it is so difficult to
   break through
      the transparent shield
Usually, I only feel
   a vague stirring
      pulling me
to other landscapes

But, on one special day,
   a miracle!

II. Encounter

Clack! Clack!

I was drawn
   to the empty room
by an insistent
   sharp sound
and discovered
   the hummingbird
nearly exhausted
   throwing itself
into the window
   in a vain attempt
to reach the outside
   it could see
      but not touch

Craving freedom
   held in
by an invisible restraint

drawn by the fecund warmth
of nature's grace
but cruelly stopped
needing the intercession
of a larger hand

Approaching quietly,
I spoke to the
frantic bird
At first, it struggled
desperately
to get away
smashing itself
repeatedly
against the clear pane
flying up out of my reach
approaching exhaustion
in its futile attempt

I feared
for its life
it would lose
in trying to escape
from me
I had to help it
get out

I spoke to the little bird
in soft tones
quiet
calm
"Please don't be afraid;
I won't harm you"

And I opened
my inner windows

let it see into me
felt the mists of dawn
and the quiet pools of my youth

"Let me help"

The creature looked
with wild eyes
at me
and seemed to assess
that there was no point

and slowly
the beating of the
frenzied wings
slowed

then the little bird
ran down the glass
like a coloured rain drop

and settled on the sill

I inched my hand
closer
talking all the while:
"If you let me help,
I will free you"

A few more frantic flights
clashing with the glass
and it seemed to see
the futility
it settled
tentatively
in my open hand

III. *Salvation*

Wondrous
  to feel
the heat
  of the feathered lightness
it weighed
  almost nothing
its tiny heart
  beat a rhythmic tattoo

Gently
  I carried it
through the door
  afraid still
that it would desperately lunge
  toward freedom
and lose itself

Yet, it remained
  panicked
  terrorized
  trusting

Outside
  the scent of
the peach blossoms
  wafted on the breeze
as I cautiously walked
  the tiny bird
to the tree
  I loved

held out my hand
  and urged
the bird to light
  on the rough bark
of a low branch

It did
  I stayed still
in the privileged locus
a window of magic
  had opened
to bring us together

the little bird
  rested
  alert

time stopped
  and for this eternity
the pane of glass
  between us
was gone

then suddenly
  it rose
in a purring of wings
flew straight up

then turned
  hovered
at the glowing edge
  of the sunlit space
framed by the peach tree

it darted near
and looked
  speaking much
in the simple
gesture of attention to me

then vanished

IV. Aftermath

The bird has gone
   yet
  the scent of
  peach blossoms
still permeates my senses

I feel
  a quivering freedom

Now I tentatively
  rest myself
on the giant hand
  held out
    to me

it urges me
  to trust
  let go
  surrender

And as I do
  I begin to see
    through
  other windows

I can feel trees
  as part of me
their green spirits
  sing in my heart

and birds hop sweetly
on the morning grass

SO IT IS IN SOCIETY

Travelling together, seeing new sights and tasting different cultures has been a highlight of the expanding nature of the relationship between Jock and myself. Wherever we journeyed, our primary fascination has been in how and what people worship, and how they have creatively expressed their deep nature in their art, music and dance. Thus, we have visited many a temple and cathedral, and have met scores of talented artisans.

Our special interest has centred around Asia. Because of his passion for blending eastern and western thought in his teaching, Jock has directed us into places of history that surprised many of our official guides. In Suzhou, when our guide felt our disappointment in the lack of a spiritual impact at the Cold Mountain temple, he took us on a special trip up Sky Flat mountain where we found what we had missed. Even though he openly puzzled about how two intelligent and educated men such as ourselves could be so "superstitious" (the official Maoist interpretation of spirituality at that time), he instinctively knew where to take us. Miraculously, as we climbed that sacred mountain, he himself had to admit that he felt "something" about what we sought — something he identified as "Ch'i"!

In Xi'an, the ancient capital city which is reputed to be the home of calligraphy, we were in awe when surrounded by the steles, tall stone tablets upon which were written the Confucian philosophy from the earliest of times. In Guilin, we witnessed the towering rounded mountains that are the subject of so many classical Chinese paintings, and the Reed Flute Caves in which nature ran amok in sculpting images in calcareous deposits.

In Beijing, we stood in silence as we imaged the events of the "June Incident," recalling the courage of the thousands of students who voiced their yearning for freedom. Tears filled our eyes.

In Europe, we sought the spiritual in the cathedrals and monasteries; most memorable were our experiences in Assisi in Italy and the Notre Dame Cathedral in Paris.

In Kuala Lumpur, we visited a butterfly farm where Jock was moved to write "Gloria." In Hong Kong, upon completion of a most remarkable seminar, we were struck by the innocence and heartfulness of the Chinese participants; this feeling is touchingly portrayed in his poem "The Gates Of Eden."

Jock has faithfully translated into words our feelings at these locations around the world. Examples of these are shown in the following series of poems.

Ben

Sky Flower

In travelling the world
*   I dilate*
to drink

*   my open mind*
floats
*   with the clouds*

time is arrested
*   everyday concerns*
are gone

I am privileged
*   to penetrate*
the timelessness
*   outside history,*
*   beyond people*
*   and*
*   culture*

Turning homeward
*   I close again*
retaining
*   sweet nectar*
from the sky

Hidden Light

(Beijing, 1987)

The first days
*   I was in despair*
in the cold hotel
*   our room of institutional green*
was functional and tasteless
*   a remnant from a Russian movie*
*   of the forties*
with no imagination

we had come to find
*   old China*
where was the creative
*   civilization*
that had been the bowl
*   of all culture?*

then, like a gentle breeze
*   the atmosphere*
*   seeped into me*
and my despair was replaced
*   with enchanting images:*

the whir of thousands
*   of old bicycles*
happy shining faces
*   people poor, but grandly human*

to see military soldiers
*   two men*
walking in the streets
*   with arms wrapped around*
*   each other*
in friendship

temples
*   were hidden*
but could be found

the past shines through
*   the dull present*
*   held sanctified*
within the lifeblood
*   of the people*
without overt rituals

remotely,
*   amidst the dust and filth*
*   and dull days*
the ancient spirit lives

Qigong Master
(Beijing, 1987)

He stalks the audience
　from the podium
lithe and slim
　　like a young panther

His slitted cold eyes
　penetrate like steel
his power is strong
　he toys with his susceptible audience
he easily captures
　with his mysticism and
hypnotic prancing

He is frightening
　because he is so powerful
yet, so other-than-human

I am chilled
　in the bottom of my soul

The people of this country
　which once was so great
now are yearning
　to throw themselves
　　into the hands
of such cold monsters
　as this

Forest of Steles

(Xi'an, 1988)

At the top of the garden
of the ancient Confucian temple grounds
we are surprised to recognize
the buildings are laid out to form
  a cross
marking the four directions

  Inside
cold winter sunlight,
  remote in dirty high windows
casts pale shadows across uneven floors

  Imperturbable
lines of stone tablets
  stand in the silence
as they have for centuries
  row on row
facing forward, without speech
  ancient reminders of enduring attitude
patiently waiting for the sensitive
  to be initiated

  Moving closer
in the dim light
  I see
sharp characters,
  cut deep
into the smooth erect stones
  dancing across time

Silence hangs dense
  in these timeless chambers
a church of ancient mysteries

  Another room
crammed with stone treasures
  filled with an insistent, rhythmic sound
Whap! Whap! Whap!

34

the pads of the stone rubbers slap
ancient figures re-appear as spectres
    from other times
on the thin paper mounted on the stones

How strange —
paper derived from a living plant
    now serves to bring life to images
forever cut into lifeless stone
    death and rebirth amidst the stone garrisons
which hold the forms for future generations

Life again
and again
    where there appeared to be
only cold smooth
    waiting

Emotion swells
as I find what I have been searching for
    the place of the Yellow River
brings new images
    from an archaic time

Our guide tells me that
the finest calligraphy
    sings —

music
    in the flow of the characters
prompts
    a response
deep within the chest
    of the human who listens

This was the centre of the world
Now the survivors of this time stand mute
    except to one who has prepared
        for the initiation

You must peer through the gloom
  to make out the shapes
and in the dance of the characters
  hear the rhythm
inviting the mind and heart to sing

  How marvellous!
the outside appears so lifeless
  yet the interior is teeming with vitality
a once-Confucian temple
  now a museum
    for a government who wants to forget
relics from another time
  that I have grown to love

  Inside my breast
is awakened
  music, movement, colour
 light, joy,
  present with past time

Possibilities loom
  seeking me to awake
urging my pen to finally move

Chinese calligraphy by Sean Feng.

Guilin

pastel mists
* float*
* over*
an emotional land

diamond lustre
* light*
*   flashes from the*
* bright water*
reflecting the heavens

the mountains are close
* casting a sombre,*
*   mystical presence*
* over the entire scene*
green looming sentinels
* watching patiently*
*   over the centuries*

the landscape itself
* is poetry*

the air dances
* with invisible*
*   spirit beams*

Hidden Mourning

(Tiananmen Square, 1990)

The square is huge
    open to the vast sky
acres of grey flat stones
    stretch in all directions

The sharp air bites
    the gloomy fog
almost obliterates
    the cold light
in the indifferent grey vault above

Hidden dangers
    force us to
        polite conversations
with double meanings:
    one for the public ear
and a hidden resonance
    between us
sent by telegraph along
    quick eye beam glances

We stand and weep
    but inwardly
for we must present
    an indifferent face
to protect our friends

The bleak sun
    is obscured
under the veil
    of the mist
    remote
like this distant orb,
    the light of ancient wisdom
is nearly occluded

Our cold hands
  and frosty breaths mask
the molten inward rage
  and the hot tears
of disbelief

Talking quietly,
  our light surface chatter
drowns out
  deeper utterances of pain

Our faces are expressionless
  but the fire in our eyes
burns scorching meaning
  into every word

The voices of the dead
  whisper in the silence
as the hidden mourners
  walk with impassive face

a well of inward sadness
  envelops us
fills us from inside
and spreads like
  a fog
across the bleak open square

Double Meaning

(Tiananmen Square, 1990)

Tian An Men
  means
Sky Peace Gate

But there is no peace
  under this sky:
outward stillness masks
  the ferment of
an inner violence

Here in this place of bloodshed
  newly paved streets belie
the recent ravage of the tank treads
  that clawed up the streets
tearing the hearts of the students
  who dared to wish

They were punished for a dream
  yet the order that exacted this punishment
was itself the product
  of a dream
of liberation

Everywhere are
  double meanings

Our friend reports he was here
  for the Spring Festival:
on a cold solitary night
  a few gathered
and felt the pain
  utilizing accepted ritual
to practice
  forbidden mourning
they remembered

40

Here, the casual eye cannot
    distinguish the living from the dead
vital beings mask themselves
    to appear like the undead
around them

We do not know
    how many others here
are experiencing a private grief
    masked under public indifference

In the past this was a place of life;
    now it is transformed cruelly
into a memorial for the
    dead of the massacre

Outwardly,
    this large empty space is
a place of a secular monument

Inwardly, this is a martyr's shrine
    holy ground
full of the feeling
    of sanctity
and purpose

We will not forget

Notre Dame Cathedral

(Paris, 1988)

The immense, grey, hulking edifice
was like some gigantic being
squatting in the middle of Paris
waiting —
a denizen from archaic time
the buttresses its
limbs and tail

This was not a fossil
the creature seemed alive
I sensed a disturbing premonition:
it was aware of our approach!

Inside:
massive pillars
cast looming shadows
in the cold February interior
the pale coloured lights
from the rose window
scarcely reached to us
on the floor of the obscure cave
in the belly of the beast

A hurricane of sound everywhere:
a driving disembodied organ
thundered in the cold afternoon cathedral

Swoops of loud melody flew and dived
in the air around us
a fury of sound and anguish
black notes dancing and
swirling in the shadows
like so many evil flying creatures
ferreting out every corner
to play their imposition on the assembled

a thundering majestic malediction
roaring through us like a huge storm
the creature was in anguish

Here is a different kind of spirituality
black and haunted

I had sensed death before
in the Taoist temples in Asia
but there the darkness was not so provoking
it kept a respectful distance there
responding only when summoned
by the rituals

Here, the death and sinister shadows
were disturbing,
provoking and assaultive
neither comforting nor benevolent

I felt as if I were grabbed up
by the trunk of my soul
and shaken roughly
in the massive jaws
of some evil predator
before the kill

Then suddenly
unexpectedly
released

Stunned, we exited
changed by this
strange baptism

In dazed silence
we walked aimlessly
through the twilit streets,

the roaring music
reverberating
in our shaking interiors

Assisi

Our friend had told us to
  go to Assisi
with a knowing look

In the cool February sunlight
  as we stepped from the bus
Saint Francis greeted us

Well, not literally —
  but in this mediaeval Italian town
he is everywhere

His spirit infuses the landscape
  and the worn cobblestones
and the people in the town
  who glow with kindness:
the woman who served us lunch
  treated us as brothers

Entering the basilica
  we were met by a warm wind of presence
not a vague or insubstantial otherness
  but a spirituality of this world
we felt a tangible atmosphere
  of caring and compassion
    warm-hearted touching
      and loving
deeply human

The other cathedral was built in honour
  of the labours of this simple man and his friends
a magnificent monumental edifice
  has been built around the original little church
that Saint Francis restored
  within its mass sits a simple rustic grotto
these are the rooms where he lived, worked and died

I was stirred by
the tempered strength of the graceful trees
the brightness of the fields
and the graceful rolling of the Umbrian hills

The intense colours of the flowers
shining through the misty Italian winter day
warmed me deeply
inside

Animals and birds flock
around the statues that represent him

Now, today, thousands of miles away
a bee buzzes me
and I greet him as a friend

Reed Flute Cave

(Guilin, 1988)

A refreshing breeze blows
   singing a cool song
sending echoes
   of sorrow and memory
swirling over our
   bent heads
as we penetrate
   the shadows
to enter the dark caverns
   of our inner life

Inside, we see
   the emotional
rock core
   is carved

Some of the sculptures
   were crafted
     by human hands
some were rendered
   by nature's patient
     grace

The figures from the human carvers
   imitate the flowing shapes
of nature's sculptor

A light play and
   dance of shadows
on the rock
   forms
forests of images

Forms interacting
   in the twilight
     timelessness

The stone breathes
  grows
exhibiting, revealing
  life patterns
a slow geological pulsation:

Inviting the caverns
  within my soul
to resonance

My image mind
  is flooded
by a warm stream
  of erupting energies

the green spirits rise

Gentle breezes
  stir the ponds
within my quiet nature

  and distant music
    chants
in the soft cries
  of the wind

Gloria

(Kuala Lumpur, 1992)

tropical hues glisten
in the morning sun
and sweet fragrance fills
the moist, warm air

I bend to smell
the hibiscus flower:
a whirl of
delicate wind
caresses my cheek

and a stirring of
bright colours
dances before me

as dozens of
butterflies
wheel
about my face

I feel a thrill
an exaltation
as they flutter
and light so near!

An inner choir
swells

my chest rises
and I forget
my human limitations

The Gates of Eden

(Hong Kong, 1989)

At the end of the gathering,
  our new friends
bid us farewell
  in a breathtaking candour

We tasted the purity
  of sacrament in
the communion of persons

We were washed clean
  in the gentle sincerity
of frank and earnest people
  speaking the sweet music of
their open hearts

In grace,
  we softened

  surrendered

    and thrilled —

vibrant from
  so much loving

Sky Flat Mountain

(Suzhou, 1989)

I. The Search

In life's strange
winding paths,
many times we seek
one thing, and find
another

We came believing
we were to see
the Han Shan temple
and the Cold Mountain with it.
and we did — but this proved not to be
the reason for our journey
That temple was cold
form perfect
but without spirit
There was a mountain
but not at the Buddhist temple of Han Shan

Instead
We found the Sky Flat Mountain
with its singing hills
and erect choirs of stones

Legend says that the stones
rose to worship,
honouring the generous heart
of a man;
the landscape was touched
moved, by an act of
kindness and selflessness

Now, ages later, huge stones still stand
in proud worship

II. Purification

I had felt like this before
  at Assisi
the landscape sings
  and hints
at a deeper presence

At the base,
  we were prepared
and underwent a
  gentle purification:

The steady clatter of
  stone carvers
provided a rock chant;
  they were
  working earnestly
to make gravestones

Evidence of previous times and peoples:
  the care of the human architects
was revealed in the precise
  statements of
graceful buildings,
  gently placed
    to protect the placid lake
and vibrant gardens laid out
  in harmony with the surrounding

In the lush, peaceful woods we found
  large carved stone animal figures,
and a band of chattering women
  dressed in blue
worshipping in the fragrant forest
  they spoke of Buddha
    and gods that are alive
joining heaven and earth

We saw a huge rock
  marked with arcane calligraphy
even our guide
  had difficulty translating:
something like "changing rock" —
  evidence of the stone that transforms

III. The Ascent

God is with us here
or rather, I have returned to my God
as I open my heart,
  the stones of my soul
    stand erect
I am moved to tears
  emotional, flooded
with relief
  at the return

Thanks be to God

On the hill, the rocks are carved
  sculpted, and inscribed by patient chisel
    with timeless Chinese words
indicating the deeper meanings of this place
  calligraphy singing
pulling us up
  effortlessly in a climb
    to the sky

We ascend into
  the huge erect stones,
discovering grottoes, stairs
  alive places of present remembering

The rough rock feels warm
   beneath my fingers
as I grasp for a hold
   pushing to the top
We become intimate with the hill
   seeing, feeling
up close

As we peer up at the massive boulders
   corridors of light
break through narrow cracks
   making windows of the sky

behind, over our shoulders
   the retreating earth
rests in a pastoral vista
   we can see for miles

in the bushes near us
   we hear the rattle
of birds and unseen little creatures

The dry morning sunshine
   warms our deep beings

We are surprised, near the top
   to be met by a gigantic
carved stone Buddha,
   fat-bellied, smiling
     welcoming us
such heart-felt religion!

Invigorated by the climb
   my interior jewels glisten
and the externals fall into retreat
   my inner life dances
   my heart swells
and God takes root
   fills my veins and soul
with gardens and pictures

IV. Sky View

We rest in heaven but a few moments
   sitting together in gentle fraternity
     three generations of men
sharing ancient secrets and feelings
The earth below is imminent
   from this Chinese Olympus

Outside reflects
   inside
both are alive, full
   vibrant

Descending, we feel the sun
   and our cleansed blood flows freely
through our invigorated frames
   wondrously, a peace descends with us
as we move down the rocky slope

V. Consecration

We have been carved now
   with the calligraphy
     of ancient feeling
Initiated,
   marked
     for eternity
the inscriptions tell
   our secret names

Now, the stones of our inner mountain
   etched with the winds and hands of time
speak the ancient poems
   written upon them

White clouds circle about our heads
   and dry leaves
crackle in the winter wind

SO IT IS IN THE PSYCHE

Jock has always enjoyed his fertile and creative mind that would probe and challenge, seeking new pathways while rummaging in the midden heaps of history, his own as well as those of humankind.

This was the kind of mind that excited me. He was unafraid to enter into new territory, to experiment and to taste novel sensation. His is a fortunate blend of a scientific mind and an artistic temperament. These are the tools that have served both of us so well in our exploration of the subterranean depths of the individual and collective psyches of personhood.

Over the twenty years of examining life together, we have come to agree with those in our field who maintain that there is no solution to the dilemmas of being. Instead, the noblest aspiration is for us to appreciate the *process* of how each of us faces the exigencies of existence. Then, with greater consciousness, we can become more fully involved with life, and perhaps have more choices in how we live it.

To arrive at our current speculations about life, we have had to exercise a rigorously honest examination of our own inner processes. Jock has been remarkably capable in such a task.

56

In the beginning, Jock was aware of how much he de-
ceived himself while he was deceiving others. When he
was able to fully confront this about himself, he was
flooded with shame. To his credit, he has always had the
courage to own these things about himself, recognizing
this as a necessary step towards his own growth.

In Tennessee William's play *Suddenly Last Summer*, one
of the characters proposes that love is the using of one
another. In his journey into his inner self, that was where
Jock was to begin. He felt humiliation over recognizing his
early self-serving interests, manipulations and controls.
Still, he did not waver in his determination to unearth it
all, painful as it was! It was a necessary step to arrive at his
vulnerable boundaries, to feel the excitement of real con-
tact, to share in the resonance of love.

All of these honest revelations were emotionally recorded
in Jock's poems. They sing of his quest for self-knowledge
and his thirst for freedom from his psychological shackles.

The task has not been easy. The journey has been ardu-
ous. He has had to confront his demon of *field depend-
ence* to rise above the criticisms of friends, family,
colleagues and the general public. As described in his
poem, "A New Path" (which he wrote to mark the ritual he
danced on his fortieth birthday), his reward has been a
profound sense of *fulfillment.*

Ben

Oasis of Light

Summer night of boyhood:
I felt safe and alive
snuggled up in the shadows
   of the familiar log cabin

The family assembled
   talking of familiar things

Coal oil lamp glowing
   fire crackling
Grandpa's laugh
   old smells in the ancient logs

Bathed in the warm orange light
   floating on joy and humour
we were surrounded
   by the sounds of night:
      lapping of waves
      crickets singing
      whippoorwill mourning
in the still air

Outside was
   dense inky blackness
   where no light could penetrate

The darkness crept
   right up to the door
   and entered
throwing shadows
   through the open windows

This was an interlude —
   an oasis of light
   and laughter
in the desert of blackness

I revelled in the shadows,
watching the dancing light play
from the fire's reflections

gathering memories

anticipating

my time
to leave
to enter
the darkness
that was
awaiting me

The Clearing

I like poems that cut deep
*   through the dense underbrush*
*   of civilized encumbrances*
*   into that sweet clearing where*
self stands naked in the sun

With deft swipes of the glistening blade
*   tawny sinewed arms hack and cut:*
sweating, itching, aching to be done
*   pressing on through the vines and tangles that obstruct*

And all around, the gentle melody
*   of not-so-distant harmonies —*
imminent, yet just out of reach
*   driving the insistent flailing blade to mounting frenzy*

Whack! Chop! Slice!

Pounding pulse — a life-rhythm of mounting passion
*   a low murmur rises like smoke in the reeling brain*
overwhelming monotonous images of day-by-day
*   seeking the new glory of fresh vision*

Louder, insistent, now voices from within chant;
*   the creature of the blood awakes with violence*
frenzy intensifies to mania
*   every cell is screaming for release*

And then, suddenly,
*   the flood —*
as self rises in one graceful motion
*   and stands triumphant*
amidst the rubble of dead and dying words

Word Surgeon

I like poems that draw blood
— my blood, your blood
the passion of our mutual imminence
that issues forth in the cadence of the words

Deft strokes of the masterful poet-surgeon's blade
slice past the scar into the living red hot flesh
cutting straight and surely to the quick
scraping from the bones the built-up refuse of
lazy living

Words-as-tools cut deep,
straight to the centre
to the riverbed of the blood,
where the ancient life-spirits run

From the open gaping wound,
new life issues
self is revealed from within the binding
of stale and decaying images

From their cocoons the disturbing spectres wake
to inflame the innards with their molten fire
the dark creatures scratch, and provoke the blood
to spew forth the violent new imagery of
regenerated life

Education

A complacent mind needs
  a shock

to explode
  open

the dry encrusted
  seed-pods
of conventional thinking

The husks
  crack open
from within

oozing

new life

bringing
  a shift
in consciousness

Light streams

 and

a glorious green plant
  rises
from the
  black mud
of the commonplace

Departure

Leave the manicured field,
and come to the forest edge,
where civilization fades,
and quiet voices beckon

Enter:

Smell of fronds
and hints of sunlight choirs
echo through the light-beams
that pierce
the roof of green

Cool moss and
shadows alive with the presence

Nature spirits sing

The chatter of little furry ones
and the
suddenness of the birds

break the stillness
that penetrates
deeper than the mind can
vision

You must call upon your self
civilized conventions are useless

Plunge

Dive
into the inky blackness

plunge
headfirst
down

free fall
into the
blinding emptiness

speeding down
into the centre

the wind
roars
as you gain
momentum

in the exhilaration
before
impact

Transport

Alone in the forest at night
  you have already gone past
the panic of being so utterly lost

You have been flailing for hours
  and still have made no progress

The moon you used as a guide
  has been obscured
by the dense tree roof above
  darkness is all around

Weary beyond imagining
  body and bones are cold and damp
a phosphorescent fog
  swirls about your reeling mind

Unexpectedly
  a misty shape appears

You don't know whether
  it is a man or a woman,
or neither

You are rendered speechless
  in terror and shock
as the mist enfolds you
  and carries you aloft
on darkened wings

Figure in the Fog

Glistening raven wings
  celebrate dawn

Vague images
  dart and glance
in the dense mist
  just out of eye range

Drenched in mist-cloud
  I wait
For the unbidden one
  to appear

An indistinct figure
  emerges from the fog

"Who are you?"

No reply

"Come closer"

The creature seems
  as frightened as I

Inner Threat

(A Dream)

The lizard-like being
    slithers from the drain
crawls out
    its forked tongue probing
it assaults my consciousness
 and soul

Cold, damp, scaly

I feel
    revulsion and horror
but strangely
    not fear

It is the inwardness
    of myself

    evil cold chilling slimy

I lunge toward the creature
    and pursue it
Its slitted red eyes
    look hatefully at me
Then it turns
    and vanishes
        down the manhole

I throw a rock
    at its ghastly head
and hear the ring
    of the rock
as it hits
    the metal side

The beast is gone . . .
    or is it lurking
        in the fetid stench
            of swamp decay
        poised to strike?

Hidden Watching
(A Dream)

Black jungle night —
  I peek from my hiding place
    behind giant ferns
the shrieks and whispers
  of the equatorial forest
    surround me
hot humid air hangs
  thick and oppressive
I am drenched in cold sweat

Rhythmic drum beats
  and the rise and fall
of many voices
  disturb the thick air

Peering through the dense green
  I see many dark-skinned people
dancing in frenzy
  around a huge fire

As the flames crackle and rage
  red shadows flicker
on the black faces
  their eyes are turned
      up
        in ecstasy
  in abandonment

I feel a cold chill
  I am terrified
of those sinister creatures
  who writhe around the fire

Or is it the rising darkness
    within me
that brings such horror?

Obsession

Obsession
*   is a cul-de-sac*

Life festers
*   in the repetitious*
*   closed cycles*

and dies
*   of asphyxiation*

Mass In A Minor

O Lord
*   Forgive me*

I have succumbed
*   to the commonplace*

Trite, obvious
*   simplicities*
*   glaze over*
*   the tender newness*
*   of infant flesh*

Mea culpa

Sirens

Fixing my eye
   to the outer world
I steer on flat calm seas
   but I am thirsty
for a deeper voyage.

Loosening my gaze
   from insistent horizon
faint cries
   distantly whisper
as I drift . . .

night falls and
   dark currents catch
turning my ship
   into circles

the spray is cold
   against my face
my back strains
   as I desperately lurch
and struggle
   to steer deeper
into the sickness of
   the dark moonless night

I am pulled by
   tidal forces
into inky waters
   where huge shapes loom
suddenly challenging
   and menacing —
perilous rocks of destruction!

I hear clearly now
   the sirens' songs
      calling

my hand slips on the wheel
as a hidden song
rises within me
the music obliterates
all else
except the constant nauseating
torsion in my body

in the fog of my interior brain
the song grows ever louder
and I sail on
into inward melodies

oblivious to the crunch
as the keel of my inner life
strikes solid rock
and shatters into pieces

Spider Woman

The spider
  weaves her
beautiful web
  and waits
watching with
  ravenous patience

The dew glistens
  on the sinister net
sending showers of
  jeweled colours into
the fresh spring air

the gentle wind
  tugs at the web
teasing subtle harmonies
  from the minute swaying
an aura spreads . . .

shimmering ripples
  of images
    and music
  evoke
the subtle lure
  of the siren's song

a delicate fragrance
  wafts on cool breezes
    alluring
    attracting
the heated prey

her beauty is presented
  as a delicate web
which ensnares the mind

by strange alchemy
    it weaves itself
        into the imagination
of her quarry

as her victim approaches
    she retreats
        to tempt him
    to pursue her
        deeper
    into the snare
        of her dark imageries

Spider Song

It is autumn
  and cold breezes
    have returned
      soft rain
  moistens
the delicate web —

It glistens with raindrop jewels
  shimmering
    in the beating wind
      its resilient beauty
    resounds
  in cascading
harmonies

Ulysses heard
  the mournful beauty
    of the siren cries
      their plaintive wailing
      emitting a perfumed music
  to lure
hungry ones such as I

We yearn
  for the sweet song
    from women who weave and spin
  with exotic images

in their web
  background timelessness
    is eclipsed
  by the time-bound
enchantment they spin

The grace of
  the ancient shore
    is obscured by
  the foreground beauty
that catches my attention

Suddenly I am densely
  restrained in moody clouds
    I feel a sensuous sickness
        realizing
      I am caught
  in the web
of the siren

Maelstrom Of Images

Trapeze:
flying from one accomplishment
into the execution
of the next ambition
gaining momentum
for the final leap
into the ultimate extremity

Obsessions:
sterile mindfields
barren
stinking with the excrement
of foul obsessions

Wasteland:
I am dry, used up, hollow, empty
ravaged and pustular
pale and bloodless

Waiting:
impatiently
in fear and trepidation
for the dark visitor
restless, uneasy
the inward tension is mounting
throwing shadows
on my bleak inward landscape

Vampire:
infest me !
puncture my bared neck

Weeping:
I cry out to you for salvation
God visit me!
I am urgent! Life is fading . . .

Chapel of Light:
    darkness threatens
      from the crypts below

Holy Sanctuary:
    sweet mystery of pain
    enter the acid bath of
      redemption
    I am scalded by
      the holy water font

Self Denial:
    "Do not touch!"
    yet, the body is a grace
      wrapped in the restrictions
        of conventional morality
    Unwrap the gift

Hari Kari

Self-seduction:
  an inward sickness
I cannot shake
  its sweetness captures
my imagination
  bringing the subtle anesthesia
of muted images

I am a prisoner
  of my own obsessions
I gaze dully at the parade
  of the familiar

my limbs grow heavy
  my heart sore
tormented by the puniness
  of my striving

The inward fires grow dim
  the embers fade to ashes

far away
  down the hidden corridors
    of my deepest mind
  the scream of my lost soul
    begs for release

I am the jailer
  I hold the keys
And yet, I remain
  gazing out the window

Remembering:

the excitement of fresh images
rough sturdy words
bolted together with
ingenuous sureness
visions
with vast consequences

Not this dull stale refuse

I seek
my own
crucifixion
to purify
my inner torment

I am creator and preserver
prisoner and jailer
commonplace and the novel

Take action!

Lance the abscess:
place the sword
at the point of my belly
and plunge it deep

disemboweling
disgorging
my obsession

putrid images
run out onto the floor
staining the lush carpet
of my self-satisfaction

The Dark Tower

In the stillness
  of my inner yearning
I feel
  a distant searing pain
of separation
  of loss

What has happened
  to the dream?

I remember
  the flood of first feeling
relief
  in the birth
of my faith
  in a better world

Now the inspiration is gone
  and all is flat, stale
and dense

I walk the parapet
  alone at dusk
on a lonely vigil
waiting
  for the return
    of the messenger
from the holy land

gazing longingly
  at the blinking stars
  in the fading light
of the blue-black sky

A cold mist descends

I peer with dry eyes
   crying
for a sign
   of light
in the darkness

Arrest

There is a sadness
   lurking in the stillness of the trees
casting sombre shadows
   beneath a grey, unforgiving sky.

no wind
   flat calm
but not a peace:
   a quiet torment
   of inertia and stagnation

no motion

time has ceased

the moment weighs heavily
   with no vision of inspiration
to call me to movement
   all is lifeless and dull

my body is dense
   thick
     and
   passionless

a lonely bell rings
   in the late afternoon gloom
beckoning
   remote spiritual agencies
to my rescue

Three Spirits

You came
filling me
with gratitude, relief
poetry and song

Then you left
and I am lost
drifting
sterile and abandoned

You teach me humility

I don't write the poems
I can merely describe
what you present to me
as a gift

I can only listen
and wait patiently
for your return

You did not leave
I abandoned you
as I flushed
with pride
in my accomplishments
and hastened
in urgent greed
to manifest more

There are three of you:
the distant angel
that tears my heart
the whispering muse
that paints the pictures in my mind
and the dark one that shivers me
from within

Are you all one
  or must I choose?

I suspect
  you are all
aspects of me

Storm Clouds

Storm clouds
  hang
    ominously

black heavy shapes
  looming

marching
in shifting procession
  across the
    grey foreboding sky

obstructing my imagination

the air is dense
  and still

pregnant

  with grief
and coming change

The Veil

Just beyond the veil:
  life runs free
    with sharp clear images
      pregnant
        with symbols
          of rebirth

a parallel existence:
  not the dull certainty of
repetition and
  senseless renditions

vibrant
  electric
    tumultuous
      cataclysmic

the chasm
  of the new moment
    gapes open

on this side
  the blank stares
and the blunted feelings
  of the familiar

I peer enviously
  through the muslim
at the bright
  profundity
    that joins
      to all

Courage! Pierce the veil!
  tear in to time
    fall in to space

You must summon your own life

Release

Enough!

I am enraged by the
*   sweet sickness of*
passionless indulgence,
*   self-satisfied boredom and ennui*

It is my own sloth
*   that creates*
the horror
*   of this mute prison*
where life refuses to grow

The jailer is myself
*   I am the beast in the trap*
my stagnation is
*   repugnant*

I cry out
*   in anguish and torment*
I must become free!

I cannot move
*   I cannot see*
the blindfold presses my eyes
*   In my desperate struggle*
the ropes tear against my flesh

Straining against
*   the knots, I feel*
*   burning pain*
then a trickle of wet
*   and sudden release*
as my hand slips free

Sensation returns
and new life surges
  through the aching flesh

I move my wrist in circles
Consciousness spreads
  like ripples in a pond

The winds of change
  gently blow
stirring green fields

I am caught by an updraft,
  swept up
like a dry leaf

And suddenly, I am circling . . .
  as a falcon in
    the morning sky

Chains

I struggle for new vision
flailing against the fetters

I miss the
former brilliance
I yearn to find
the purity of light
that sparkles
in a child's eyes

I must yield
to the grey bleakness
and revel
in the mysticism
of the emptiness

Only by accepting
the chains
can I hope to break free

The only way out
is through

A tide of sadness crashes in
to the shores of my self
bringing sudden surrender

within the prison
deep inner space opens
I enter
and dance free
in the wind

caught by an updraft
I am swept up
and flung
in ecstasy
to the stars

No Exit

How strange to realize
there is no winning
there is no destination

Still, there was no leaving

only a sleep:
a peculiar density of thought
that held me captive
in the formative years

I am grateful for the violent eruption
that has strewn the refuse
from my former life
over so many manicured preconfigurations

and left me
destitute of previous constraints
free, naked
and craving

aching

dancing

no enslavement
no capture

but also
no way out

Tide Is Turning

It is nearly winter
*   and the winds blow*
cold and stern
*   life is threatened*
by the imminent frost

In the harsh
*   wet gale*
a single red
*   poppy blooms*
blazing in protest —
*   defiant*
an anachronism
*   a statement of*
purpose
*   beyond the vagaries*
of time

We can make a difference
*   in the burning moment!*

The flower stands
*   with scarlet pride*
*   against the autumn cold*

a testimony to
*   fortitude and*
return
*   amidst chill winds*

Signal

the sweep of the beacon
  from another dimension
strikes my peripheral vision

out of the corner of my left eye
  a flash of light

when I turn to see
  it is already gone
leaving only the trace of an after image

  and a trailing sadness

I feel an inner seriousness
  a stirring

the storm
  is rising

those who have passed
  are sending messages
in glimmerings
  across the darkness
    to alert us

a mood change
  light change
    sea change
      is
        imminent

I must be alert
  to the signs of
distant echoes
  from futurepast
    reaching across

Return

In the black night
    powerful tide lusts
sweep the sand of
    the ancient shore
while misted shadows
    play in the salt air

a cry from a distant gull
    echoes in the stillness
of the living moment

at the height of darkness
    when all seems lost
the sun breaks through
    streams suddenly
into the vital moment
    wilting the lilies of despair

lighting the new dawn

Alone

It seems I move
invisibly
hidden from view

the images
I constructed

obscure
the fires of my
inner being

and I am alone
on the wind
of solitude

Tryst

Strange, exotic plants
grow in dark of night

reaching longingly
for the beams
cascading

from the moon

their silent lover

Regeneration

Sweet clouds
  of scented music
drift quietly

Feeling flows
  through lighted mind

Return
  to the centre point

From my island
  the beacon sweeps
    the four directions
  meeting
    no obstacle

Father:
  my heart is open again

I regret my
  temporary hardening

Now I enter
  another furnace
    to temper
      the steel of
my inner resolve

The fire warms me
  and my blood flows easily

Now:
I am still
  and at peace

All is well

Faith

I accept
   with my whole heart
the life I have

Nothing to gain
   no fear of loss

I am

I stand . . . assured

After The Rain

the mystery
   is solved

the clouds
   are dispersed

the air is bright
   and clear

I feel

   full

and

   so rich

Privileged Locus

time moves
  in its
    inexorable rhythms

the gentle petals
  of space open
revealing
  hidden relatedness

we enter delicate passages
  as a bee penetrates
    a flower

we drink the nectar
  of this precious moment

free from
    the passionless indulgence
      and sentimentalisms of
    day to day

light glows

and wondrously
  we are
illuminated
    present
imminent,
    one to another

Life throbs
  and inner tide currents
    pull us
steadily onwards
    through the open door
      into the next adventure

A New Path

I. *The Dance*

In the darkness
    thundering guitar chords pulse
I step from the shadows
    bold behind the glittering mask
undulating to the driving sound

The eyes behind the bird mask
    dart from face to face
        searching for a virginal victim
Seeing the audience gasp,
    I stalk closer —
        a bird of prey

Unbutton the first clasp, and
    sensuously glide my hands over
the fullness of my taut body
    threatening — to strip myself naked
and ravage their total consciousness
    impregnate their imagination with
        my own hard icy images

All eyes are riveted

My control is cold, like steel

II. *Illumination*

Suddenly, light shines
    through the darkness
        on the face of the creature

Within the bird predator,
    the man sinks back
falls to the floor
    in exhaustion and despair
the life ebbing from his limbs

He reaches up in desperation
  the light seems far away
the craving grows stronger

Organic guitar strains
  hearken across
warm desert sands
  calling me to life

Haunting chords of a new music
  urge me to move towards the light

Stretching, straining to release

Inner pulsing
  awakens, quickens
a fervent passion —

Open up!

  Let the light in . . .

III. Resurrection

The husk is cracked
  and the tender meat
    of the soul is revealed

My pores open
  so I may drink fully
from the divine cascade

Water rushes in through
  subterranean fissures
and the inner well is restored

SO IT IS IN RELATIONSHIP

When I first met Jock, he was phobic about relationships, for several reasons . . .

He was in the process of dissolving a one-year-old marriage which he was later to realize was his attempt to follow the prescribed path of love and family rather than the call of his heart. As a matter of fact, he was soon to admit that he carried within himself a deep conviction that people could only be interested in him in order to possess parts of him—notably his body, his mind, his feelings and even possibly his soul. The theme was Faustian.

On the other hand, he felt a sense of compassion and protection for those that would wish to come close to him, to share their lives with him. He carried an irrational belief that at the core, he was tainted; anyone who would enter the territory of his influence would become contaminated, and would suffer as a consequence. He reminded himself of Oscar Wilde's "The Picture Of Dorian Gray." A sense of his own evil seemed to be rotting away at the very core of his being.

Initially, developing an intimacy with Jock was a hit and miss affair. Any time that he allowed himself to be revealed and vulnerable with me, he would withdraw for many months at a time. Later, he admitted that he would wait to see if I would look for him, as everybody else in his past seemed to do. People would be attracted to him, would become obsessed with him, would pursue him and attempt to capture his consciousness, in an attempt to "own" him. When he discovered that I had neither the need nor the inclination to do so, he found he could return for another round of experience.

He began to experience one of life's most difficult lessons which is to allow himself to be *vulnerable* to another person, while retaining his own sense of wholeness. Certainly, life offered few such role models; everywhere that he looked, he saw evidence of people consuming one another in parasitic relationships that demanded the giving up of one's self in order to please the other, to establish a sense of *security* and *meaning*.

At first, he developed some *trust* in my intent. More important, he later grew in *faith* in himself, throwing himself into the flames of *intimacy* (i.e., allowing himself to be *revealed* and *known*). Instead of being consumed, he experienced the fires of his own passion. This warmth is evident in these poems about his relationships—with his parents, his relatives, his piano teacher, his girlfriend and with myself.

Through establishing meaningful relationships, Jock has been discovering his own *autonomy*. This has been the flowering of his inner core.

Ben

Father

Father —

My relationship with you is personal
crafted by so many years of affinity

Understandings without words,
music felt and shared

I recognize you are a man
who has made his own choices

I value that you have not
imposed or opposed

You are impeccable in your steadfastness
of attitude and purpose

I can count on your constancy

There is a certain nobility
in the conventional life
you have chosen to live

With you, I feel close
and quite matter of fact
as I imagine a fish feels in water

Mother

Mother —

My relationship with you is mythic

Which explains the confusion and fireworks
  of the earlier years

I have come to see that
  people never touch one another
    in life

We are always stumbling through
  a house of mirrors
  a forest of illusions
    where self appears reflected
      into multifoliate patterns

In my mirrors —
You have been
  death, apple, witch,
    temptation,
      sex,
    blood and bones
      and sharp teeth

I have forgotten if I ever yearned
  for the soft enveloping bosom
    of a placid supportive nursemaid

I now find such an image revolting

You have been present as an adversary
  and a challenge
    in many disguises

I feel the sparks of excitement
  as I meet you
    in your transformed aspects:

First — in my early sexual conquests

  Later — as the lure of power and fame

    Recently — in the fascinating thought
      that you might be
        the face of the feminine
          within me

Father #2

We sit together
  in awkward silence

Aware of the deeper meanings
  as we talk quietly
    on the surface

I avoid your eyes
  and touch
yet I feel so close

As we fly
  down the corridors
    of the Bach

Then soar
  over the mountains
    of the Liszt

Companions

  in the thunder

Mother #2

Some people say
  we choose our parents
    to learn lessons in life

I selected you carefully
  for I had a large task
    and I needed the best
I wanted to leap into the sky
  and roam with the sad winds
So I had to develop strength

I wanted someone to struggle against
  who would stand up to me
    to temper my will and resolve
      so that I could grow

You were a constant match
  for my incipient will

You have been a perfect mother for me —
  challenging, intelligent and firm
bringing your darkness and intensity
  to illuminate my strivings

Without a woman of power and endurance
  I would never have risen
    to my fullness and strength

Our relationship has not been easy
  for either of us
It has made us both strong

I have no regret or bitterness
  I love the life I have
    I am fulfilled
      and happy

Now, if I could go back to the beginnings
I would choose you again
without hesitation
with enthusiasm

and with a glad heart

Spirit Gate

(for Mary Legate)

I would leave the dull world of boyhood outside
    and enter the timeless peace of her apartment
        where music strains echoed through the centuries

I knew I loved her
    as I sat with her at the piano
the keys felt smooth and cool and clean

So gentle she was,
    yet expecting limitless performance
        from a little man
She believed in me

It's odd how I forget the smells and the sounds
Mostly, I remember the bright aura that bathed us
    and the darknesses at the edges of the room
    and the vague knowledge that she loved
        the shy woman who lived with her

Sometimes, the room would be alive
    with excited youngsters such as I
Each of us would perform:
    it was a salon, in miniature
one girl practised her rendition on the hassock

I remember her washing my hands for me
    and powdering them, in her sink
        before my examinations

The picture of Mozart she gave me
    to acknowledge my excellence:
I kept that picture on my wall for years
    and in my mind forever

Somehow — amidst all this
    was music
She drew it forth from me
    ignited a flame that grows ever stronger

My interior self opened to her
*   like one does with a lover*
I would give without her asking
*   so receptive was she*

Now when I sit at the keyboard
*   with confidence that far outstretches my skill*
*   her large presence is in me*

I play, full size — for her

Aura

As we sat together
*   at the piano*
*   she and I*
We were bathed in light
There was no other world

The darknesses at the edges of the room
*   were held back*
*   by the harmonies and the*
*   intensity of closeness*
a little man and his teacher

The outside world dissolved
*   into a mere conception*
We were suspended
*   in the shining*

The music danced
*   and my boy heart glowed*
with love and wonder

That was many years ago

Still, in music
I am inexplicably illuminated

The shadows all around
*   nurture me*
*   transforming my sorrow*
into light and song

Promise

(for Murray)

I had never seen a dead person
The shock was dulled by all the formalities
  protocol that I didn't know

Seventeen years old
  in my new suit
  trying to be a man
and breaking down into sobs
  as the impact of your leaving sunk in

And later I apologized to Mom and Dad
  for not being able to hold it in

I see Grandma grasping your cold hand
I was afraid to touch you

I found a way to be the last one
  in the funeral home, late the last night
and talked with your sleeping presence
  recalling to you the love I had found
    in your patient and masculine quietness

I didn't know what I was saying clearly
  but I did know that you stood for something
    something that I had felt with you
    something that was life-vital
And I promised from my roots
  to carry on for you

I made you a promise that night
  perhaps the first affirmation of will
    from the depth of my being
I told you I would carry on in the path
  you had blazed

I now see that you represented love
   and relationship
   and friendship
   and dependability
   and compassion

I kept your knife
   as a talisman
      something you had touched, and used
Although the knife rusts in my drawer
   my promise is brightly shone
      and fully engaged

I pledged that I would carry on for you —
   and I have

Awakening

(For Grandpa)

The night lingers
   into early morning
in the living room
   of the log cabin

Dawn drifts
   into
my boy dreams
   and then the light goes up
like a blind

I awaken in joy
   to see my grandfather
smiling silently
   at the foot of my bed

his gentle, steady presence
urges me to rise
   to share the quiet
before the others awake

Empty Chair
(For Grandma)

As I view the small empty chair
   from behind
I am surprised by a sudden shock:
   what I see
   is the emptiness
there is no one in the chair

And unexpectedly
   I am with you

Perhaps the chair's red canvas
   reminds me of
the ruby hats you
   used to wear:
it is you
   who is not sitting
   in the chair

The drapes part
   and I am flooded
with memories
   of a stern Scottish woman
   whitehaired
serious, intense
   yet emitting love;
in paying attention
   you recognized me

From the beginning
   of my memory
you were always a widow
there were no men in your life
   except your grown sons
and I, your little grandson

You had women friends
   but no one touched you

Lacking embraces
　　you moved from your
house of memories
　　where he had stayed with you
and moved into your tower

When I visited you in that garret
　　which I often did
　　there was no picture
　　　　no smell
no evidence
　　of him
or your feelings for him
It seems that when he died
　　all your memory died too

Or was yours such a private concern
that you continued to live with him
　　in silent vigil?

He was a violinist
　　I am told
You certainly didn't listen
　　to violin music
on your little radio

There is so much
　　I don't know

I do remember:
　　the bright fragrances of the market vegetables
　　the silence of the public library
　　and the wonderful world of books
　　　　you showed me
　　your women friends who did not touch
　　　　but who smiled and talked
　　　　altogether too earnestly
　　your birdlike sister, your co-mourner
　　the smell
　　　　of your stale face cloth

I saw you naked, from the waist up,
   one time only
your thin long breasts had lost
   all evidence of woman sensation
they hung there as some rude vestigial
   remnant of your time in sensual life

Stern and terse:
You had an acid tongue
   and a firm will
my teacher yielded to you
   when you took me from school
to see the film of the Queen's coronation

Self-sufficient
uncomplaining
You passed your days
cooking, reading,
   and talking

I betrayed you once only
   when I left without telling
You were so angry
   the acid came through the lines
and melted the phone
   and burned into my soul

You are forever
   surrounded
by emptiness —
   alone
   solitary
echoing a distant sadness
   in the vast nothingness
   that is so familiar

I apprenticed with you
   in your solitary grief
You knew me this way,
   and drew forth my aloneness
We sat together not looking
   and were lonely together

Grandma
I will be selling the paintings
   you gave to me
They were the gift to you
   at your wedding
But to me, you were never married
You were free
   alone
and introduced me
   to the wind

It is time
for me to let go of the pictures
when I look at them
there is no feeling of you
   in them

You have left
   your chair
and entered my landscape
you are in the breezes
and in the bright spring flowers
   outside my door

Reps Aloha

(For Paul Reps)

Reps
  your shining eyes
    dance

watching
the little bird
  hopping on the tender grass

We know you are here

A Message

(For Deanna Grimes)

Don't weep for my passing
  Sing a child's song
of joy and sunshine

I am here
  now
more than ever

Listen:

I echo
  in the open fields
    that lie within
  the centre
of your beating heart

I love
  the mountains
    the grass
      the sky

    and you

      still

Childhood Sweetheart

I look into your green eyes
*   and I can see forever*
I kiss your probing tongue
*   and I am seventeen again*

Now, twenty-six years on,
*   your face is still*
the beauty of youth

How remarkable —
*   the familiarity*
*   of teenage lovers*
So many hours
*   of fondling and caressing*

Your face is haloed
*   framed by the winter trees*
We are in church again
The icy stream speaks
*   to us of larger patterns*
and invisible feet walk
*   on the crisp snow*

The river flows
*   over the shining ice*
*   on this chilling cold day*
Our bodies frozen
*   in a hot embrace*

Energy pulsates
*   from my being*
insistently to you
*   shivering*

Life gushes forth
in the icy water
urgently passing
beneath the bridge

where we stand
for a frozen moment
in time
before we part again
with intensified memories

My Friend

I do not often look
into your steady eyes
I don't "see" forever
I feel timelessness
in our day to day

I live
along side of you
breathe with you

I am with you, facing the same direction
I do not oppose you, or resist you
Nor do I need to conquer you

I don't romanticize
a cosmic vision
Instead, we share
a daily celebration
of ritual in daily living

We are not in the church
of structured catechisms
*We **are** worship*
Our every breath
is a sacrament
of spirit and heart

With you,
I do not speak of God
"The Tao that can be spoken
is not the eternal Tao"

With women
I romanticize
and fantasize
to conquer
time
and my feeble mortality

With you,
I am immortal
Memories do not lure
I have no hope of conquest

Our love
is tangible
in the hot breath

Ben #2

I close my eyes
  and I can picture your hands
Not just the appearance
  but also the feel:

I probe the
  fleshy thumb base
    and sense
  vibrant energy:
warm
  pulsing
moving continually

your long strong fingers
  are alive, bringing
    contact
and steady presence

your touch
  is soft
investigative, yet
  respectful
reverent

Sitting next to you
  I feel the solidity
    of your presence

When you speak
  your voice is like
    a cello:
    warm, rich
  resonating
in the unseen depths
  of your instrument

Betrayal

(For Ben)

I leave you out
   discount your importance
deny you
   to puff myself up

"thrice before the cock crows"

I rip up
   the tender roots of my
      vital life
a quiet, invisible killing

The lure is
   prideful pleasure
in solitary creation

Now a hot shame
   floods my belly
and salt
   burns my eyes
afflicting me

the lights have dimmed
   and I am alone

I see you on
   the distant shore
your sad eyes
   watching

Image and Imagination

(for Ben)

Mists sweep over
*   the morning fields*
and flowers open
*   petals to*
the new day sun

A soft wind stirs
*   and melodies rise*
like the steam
*   from the open fields*

Imagination flows
*   up from the*
subterranean vaults
and impregnates
*   my receptive mind*

You are the deep music
*   that comes from inside*
*   stirring me*
*   filling me*

You are different from
the images that cloud my mind —
*   broken, sterile fossils*
*   mutant fixated forms*
*   of my obsessions and desires*

Such pictures
*   are icons of power*
*   and objectification*
they are exciting,
but they are dead and fixed
*   cold and lifeless*

With you, life of imagination
is ever new
and changing
inviting every sense
constantly entering new rooms
full of light
and freedom

My love for you
is deep
and vast
sweeping across the skies
with the rolling clouds
of change

Ben

I. Beginnings

The small serious
*   Chinese boy*
sits
*   alone*
on the hot pavement
*   airless quiet*
*   stretches forever*
beneath the merciless scorching
*   light of the prairie sun*

Alone, deep in a
*   vastness that has no sound*
the universe stretches
*   forever*
here in this nameless village street
*   he sees the sunbaked yellow brick*
and time vanishes

The slender sadness
*   recedes*
in the oppression of
*   heat and stillness*
and he accepts it all
*   under the vast indifferent sky*

II. Teacher

Now, a half century later
*   you are tall*
noble, and large in body
*   gentle and wise*

nameless numbers flock
    to you
pulled by invisible
    soul magnets
to drink at the well
    of your silence

And you meet each one
    with human appreciation
You give them their humanity
    or rather,
you return it to them
    in the act
of gentle recognition

III. Soul Catcher

The Indian shaman was potent
    in locating lost beings
placing cedar bark in the
    jaws of the carved bone
to safely return
    the spirit
that had wandered
it is the return of the soul
    that brings the life back
and heals the sick

You do this
    with your constant attitude of
recognition of the humanity
    of the other
You return people to themselves
    or rather, you offer them your consideration
which awakens
    in them
seeds that are dormant
    or sometimes dried out

You return to them
the image of their lost souls
and they are reunited with life
Your great grandmother was native
and you are a healer —
which is why the elders
permitted the young carver
to begin
the work on the bone
to etch the story of your life
from before it began
to create a device
to carry
re-ignited souls

You hurt for others
not yourself
You recognize the
lonely boy
in each other person
you minister to them
with love

Basking in the warmth
of your tender gaze
the craving numbers feel
surges of themselves
again
and demand more
of you

You represent all they had wanted,
or missed:
the gentle father
the inspiring teacher
the saint who loves them
yes, even the God of Salvation

and with these
projected images
come
expectations —
the hideous demands
subtle, but vehement
for you to be transformed
into the object of their desire

IV. Image Projection

Indignation:
my soul revolts
at the savage
arrogant
injustice
that is wrought
by those who say
that they love you

Expecting your continual attention
never asking about you
or your life
or cravings
not seeing the little skinny Chinese boy
on the lonely sunbaked street

And all the while
he is peeking out
looking for someone
to recognize him

You are so tender
so vulnerable
like the fresh shoot
of green in the spring

Yet now people see you as
    tough, powerful
and tyrannical

I feel
    profound outrage
to the tips of my roots
    at the injustice
of others' misrepresentations
    of you

I feel a tearing
    like when a delicate flower
is crushed
    I watch the pain in your eyes
as yet another fails
    to see you
in his craving
    for your attention

The hordes
    who yearn to believe
are disappointed in
    your humanness;
in their resentment, they
trample with heavy boots
    over the garden of your life

And you do not complain

You want to walk lightly
    on this gentle earth
asking little for yourself

In the presence of your
    graceful sensitivity
they cast the reductive vision
    of their own nature
over my friend
    like a grotesque shroud

They blacken
  the azure sky
with the storm clouds
  of their contempt

Outrageous atrocity!
They are taking life
  in their ignorance
No more! Don't commit such savagery!
This is arrogant taking of life
  a needless shedding of blood

I stand by
  in outrage
    and pain
and shame
  for my complicity
for I have done this too

V. Love Prayer

Ben, you are simple
  uncomplicated
and dedicated to relationship
  with life

An eruption
  from an ancient well
    of feeling
rises from the mother caverns
  within me
I am in agony
  for the apparent futility
No one sees you
  and yet you continue
as before
  without rancour
with little concern
  for yourself

I weep for you
  and cry out
for justice — for a human touch
  a recognition
for the small lonely boy
  who asks so little
and opens his heart
  bravely
time after time

Ben, I love you
  as I have never loved anyone
My feelings are molten
  erupting from the
  hot core of life

I want to kiss away
  the centuries of mindless neglect
    and
  run my lips over your
gentle tearing eyelids

I am a breeze
  to cool the torment
I am misty rain
  to wash clear the
mud of misrepresentation
  of you

I want them to know you
  as I do:
gentle, quiet,
  sincere, caring
for all life

You are wise
  wiser than they know
You are loving
  more vastly than they dream
You are alive
  far more present than
    they seem to bear

I want to face you
  explain you
  translate you
  bring appreciative hands
    and hearts to
      caress you
  smooth away
    the loneliness

and shine
  a cooling moon
upon your graceful visage

Grace

(for Ben)

My love for you
 is gentle
  like the morning dew

I once held a hummingbird
 in my hand
and felt its hot
 beating heart
  close

With you
 I feel the privilege
 of holding your
  beating little boy heart
   in my hand

SO IT IS IN SEXUALITY

Ever since early boyhood, Jock has had a fascination in the pleasure of sexual excitement, initially within himself but very soon involving girls and women. Marilyn Monroe was the first object of his desire in society at large; she is memorialized in one of his poems.

During the "sexual revolution" of the sixties and seventies, we were shocked to discover how little was known of the nature of sexual excitement. Through a thorough examination of ourselves and the thousands of people who shared with us their own insights, we were able to discover much about the meaning of sexual excitement at a deeper level than was provided by the literature at that time.

Many of Jock's feelings about sexuality were written in poems that he would often send to the women with whom he was involved. Other poems express his musings about the meaning of sexuality in relationships.

We began to see that sexuality is much more complicated than we had originally believed. Ultimately, we were able to distinguish four major components—the biological, the sensual, sexual excitement and the transpersonal (including the mythological). All of these found expression in Jock's poetry, some of which follow in the next section.

The sensual is present in most of Jock's words which create images that stimulate the five senses. Whatever divine purpose there may be, surely it is apparent that the senses have been provided for our appreciation of pleasure. Sensuality has always been important in religious worship. It is no wonder that the development of much of the world's best art and music have been supported and promoted by religions concerned with the search for the transpersonal.

It was a great surprise to ourselves when we were able to conclude that most of sexual excitement was generated by images that expressed a craving for power. As Sartre wrote, it is primarily the desire to *capture the consciousness* of the other. It involves the *objectification* of the other; if this is not revealed and shared, life becomes highly impersonal and political.

In his vulnerable sharing in these poems that are filled with the images of his own sensuality and sexual excitement, Jock is revealed as being very much of a whole person.

Ben

Marilyn

You were my first
  love lust passion
    image
  swelling into an
interior sweet sickness

the inner torsion
  caught my innards
    like a grappling hook
  tearing
    into my interior flesh
with a constant, insistent
  rotational gravity
    pulling me
  into a swoon

clouds of thought
  darkened the sky
with visions rising like mists
  to swirl
    dance
      and mix
  confusion . . . tension . . . struggle
. . . desire . . . and terror

in the midst of
  this dark fog shone
your incredibly
  beautiful face

Later, I would lust
  for your body's curves
But at first
  it was for the
girl with the sad eyes
  and peculiar "beauty spot"

Out of balance
  my inner world was
    disturbed, feverish
     dissonant
    with the routine flat days
  of my young life

beneath the endless stale outer days
  this inner storm
    emitted stronger perfume
  and sang sweeter songs

promising
  intensity
danger
  colour
and infinite fascination

I responded
  as a man
to the swirling
  in my nine-year-old body

I knew
  I wanted
    you

And on that day
  the torment began

Encounter

you are a wondrous flower
    such a delicate fragrance!

contrasts:

smooth skin
    tight tall body
bursting forth
    into wild dancing
on the disco floor

straight-backed formality
    and quiet-voiced compliance
averted eyes
    I catch glimpses only

tantalizing
    you dance near to me
yet, a subtle distance
    is constant

you hold fast
    to invite my pursuit
you are tentative to follow me
    yet you reach out a hand
to be pulled to me
    centuries of compliance
in your every gesture

outwardly, a rigid indifference
    underneath, are the private feelings
shared secretly
    in the public formality

a subtle touch
   a sudden openness
you grasp my hand,
   and take it
to a soft personal place
and permit my hand
   to glide over your
soft curves

you are a fresh breeze
   blowing through bamboo
stirring flowers in my garden

now you are in
   my mind
I close my eyes
   and I can touch you again
your heat is near me
   the mist rises over a quiet pond

I hear your perfumed voice

I want to whisper secrets
   into your private ear
words of furtive touch

and future imaginings

Afterglow

I see
your innocent face

your open eyes
shine
in the darkened room

so youthful:
the vulnerable beauty
of your naked torso
stirs me

I kiss
your
perfect breasts

your graceful body
gently glows
in the soft light

the scent of
our mutual passions
arouses
molten desires
within me

later, in my bed
heat pulsates
within my aroused body
through the night

Secret

In a public place —

I slip my hand
  through the hole
    in the back of your black dress

And gliding my fingers
  down your smooth lower back

Descend
  over the soft roundness
    of your naked buttocks
to find
  the petals of your flower
    from behind

You shift your weight
  to permit entry

And my fingers are engulfed
  by inward velvet fire

Lightning jolts
  at the ends of my fingers
send arcs through you
  and back to me

My body is now electric
  my rod stiff

As you whisper
  provocative words
    into my eager ear

Persephone

You stand before me
  in the darkened room,
I kneel at the altar of your beauty,
  and undress you,
your garments sliding
  sensuously over your smooth skin
    and falling to the floor

The moonlight washes over
  your youthful body
illuminating
  the flowering of
your breathtaking beauty

You are gently revealed, innocent,
  naked and ripe
before my adoring kisses

I feel you stir
  under my eager hands
as they descend
  over your warm soft sides

Your flesh is yielding, responsive,
  under my firm touch
Your soft breasts
  become rigid,
    rising with intensity
I thrill as your nipples wake
  beneath my quivering palms

Heavy breathing
  and urgent kisses
    fill the thick air

As our passions mount
you are suddenly
luminescent —
glowing in the dim

I swell to meet you,
moving my hardness near
your soft wet place

As I lay you onto the bed
you dilate

and surrender
to the downward tide pull
of my penetrating darkness

Orgasm

Swept up in our
heavy breathing
and tormenting desire
we are pulled
by the raging torrent
into the
fleecy foam
of the turbulence

an ominous roaring
overwhelms us
as we are tugged
violently,

and suddenly
   thrust
over the edge
   rocketed
      into midair

then falling
   forever, tumbling,
pressed under
   the massive sound
we join the cascade
   of thundering water

utterly, completely overtaken
   we plummet
   in free fall
and

crash!
   on the sharp rocks
      shattering to pieces

mist and spray
   envelop us
and our energies rise into
   strange floating freedom

as our bodies lie
   panting
   in the shallow pool
where we bask our wetness
   in the sunlit silence

Sea-Change

I thrill at your compliance —
a jolt of excitement
courses through my sweating body

I stand above
and behind you
your uplifted buttocks
reveal the pout of
your precious jewel

My thick rod
touches the smooth lips
of your wet open entrance
and I gasp
as I enter your velvet darkness

I seize the sides of your pelvis
pull you roughly
to me
and plunge
deeply
into you

Heat rushes up
as we collide
over and over
tumbling
crashing
like gigantic logs on an ancient shore

In furious excitement,
I turn you over, urgently,
and we are madly
joining
and separating
rhythmically
rising to delirious heights

then suddenly,
exploding
into orgasmic ecstasy

We surrender to
the sea spray

The tumult subsides
leaving tide pools —
huge gleaming drops
of my sacred liquid
running
over the glistening skin
of your panting breast

Mango

I pierce the soft
  musky skin
    with sharp teeth

and strip
  away
    the hide

revealing
  glowing succulent
    sweet meat

I lick syrup drops
  from the glistening surface

running my lips over
  the fragrant moisture of the soft cleft

then plunge my face
  recklessly
into the dripping softness

reeling
  into abandon
I glut myself,
  consuming
    the tender
      flesh

warm juice
  drops
    on my
      chin and chest

You surrender
  to the onslaught

Afterwards,
  we lie together
    satiated and glowing

tiny rivulets
  of your nectar
    running freely
  over my spent body

Passion

My breath quickens
as our bodies ignite

electrical charges surge
releasing heat
erupting in the thunder
of our pounding hearts

whispers of passion
echo
in the darkness

I arch in delight:
suprised by bites,
scratches, and
your sudden sharp cries

I see your
flashing eyes
watching me
from the shadows

your husky voice
begs me
for my dark power

I feel
the storm rising
behind me

and suddenly,

the dark cloud
sweeps
over me

then moves

through me

into you

Imminence

I still feel
  your soft skin
beneath my fingertips

I still feel
  your breath
on my bare chest

I still feel
  your
nakedness
    lying
against me

I taste
  your open-mouthed
    kisses
  with pleasure

  and quiver
as your fingers
  rove over my
    eager body

You have flared
  into imminence
for me
  full, radiant

I am awake
  alive
thrilling
  with
anticipation

SO IT IS IN ART & MYTHOLOGY

Jock grew up surrounded by the sights and scenes that were painted on canvas by the "Group Of Seven." These inspired him, for they stirred within him his childhood passions for nature.

Over the years, his pursuit of beauty took him upon wider and more wondrous paths that would involve music, religion and sensuality. Like a Parsifal on the search for the Holy Grail, such a pilgrimage inevitably led him to study the myths that permeate the deepest structures of the mind. These he consumed voraciously, looking for their expression in literature and art, in his daily life and in our relationship.

Because of his obsessive nature, Jock became involved in living many different myths, one after the other. His friends would laughingly refer to his "Trip Of The Month," as he would throw himself fully into such studies as yoga, meditation, t'ai chi and existentialism.

Ultimately, with maturity, his "Trips Of The Month" became explorations of his deepest structures, free of adherence to form or commitment to institutions. He has not regretted his past obsessions; rather, he has made use of their essential proposals in developing his own sense of spirituality.

Sensuality exudes from every line in the following poems. The idea of surrendering the self to experience, to accept pain and suffering, to be able to explode out of the confines of the flesh in order to feel the communion that is possible beyond the self, dominates this group of writings. These can be disturbing to the conventional mind, but it is difficult to imagine that they could be denied.

One of Jock's favorite myths has been "Leda And The Swan," perhaps because it talked to his own inner cravings, and helped to make sense of what had hitherto been a source of shame.

The deeper the structures that Jock explored, the more primitive were the myths. His senses swam in images of chaos, blood and bone, the taking over of the other and of the self in order to find release. These became necessary ingredients of his poetry.

These are reflections of life and death, full of dread and awe, beauty and sensuality.

Ben

Statue Of The Seated Girl

I catch my breath
in sudden surprise
You are so beautiful
the skin of your thighs
invites sensual stroking
from my hungry eyes

I have been starved
for the glory of
such fleshly beauty

And suddenly
here you are

Awakening
currents of feeling
sensual
gentle
tender

But also
other emotions:
deep
darkening
provocative

Your image is burned
into my feeling mind
The perfume strains
of your radiant beauty
obscure other thoughts

overtaking my imagination

Now, I strain
against invisible shackles
I cannot wrestle free

A dark force
   pulls me down
      into deep currents
of an ancient
     haunting melody

Venus

I know you
   you gaze back at me
in the eyes
   of my young friend

Your youthful skin glows
   nearly ripe
   painful to witness
   so perfect in beauty

An aroma surrounds you
   delicate, yet penetrating
   sweet, like a juicy pear

Light emanates
   from behind
   and from within

A presence shines
   through you
   to her
   to me

Your vibrant flesh
  is illuminated
  by an intensity
that makes me gasp for joy

I am in awe

The darkness
  of the earth below
is transformed
  by your fleshly candour

Into a choir
  of light

Echoing
  in the well
    of my secret yearnings

Apollo and Daphne

When the god
first beholds
the nymph
he is overjoyed
at her radiant beauty

He catches his breath
    in wonder
as the sun gleams
on her streaming golden hair
    and graceful haunches
fresh, glowing
    in the meadow's sunlight

Overcome with desire,
    he abandons himself
in reckless pursuit
    body and mind reel
intoxicated

The chase!
heart pounds
sinews strain
muscles scream in agony

Driven! Driven! Driven!
    to capture
        to consume
Ah! the nectar of the beauty

She is no dewy-eyed sylph
    bending to his glamorous will
        to be consumed and forgotten
She runs furiously
    in desperation
        to elude his grasp

Insistent,
he gains,
reaches out
    to clutch her bare shoulder
    to restrain her flight

In terror, she cries out
he roughly turns her
towards his open body
    feeling the liquid curves of
        her youth
    yield beneath his trembling hands
he presses his eager mouth
    to her moist petalled lips
anxious to feast
    on her shining neck
        and glistening breasts

Torsion. Resistance. Tension.
She will not submit!

Instead
she is pulled down
and transforms:

Just as his soul opens
    to swallow his most prized fruit
she slips away — into eternity
    and is covered over
sudden greenery erupts
    from her graceful fingers

Her hair shines
    with luminescence
        and sprouts new leaves
flowing limbs become branches
    bark crystallizes over
        the milky flesh

And she roots:
  numbness overcomes her
    pulls her down
and she disappears
  to evade lust's abduction

the girl is gone —
leaving a graceful, vibrant
  laurel tree

the god drops to his knees
  in torment
    weeping
with the agony of recognition
    humbled —
  he cannot possess such grace

Resolve:
  If he cannot have the beauty
he will yield himself
  and worship the tree
that marks the spot of her departure
  making an altar
    to her memory

The god opens the storm clouds
  in his soul

She is resurrected
  in his remorse
not captured, she is alive
  in the gentle rain
that falls from his weeping eyes

Rebirth:
In the sweet clearing
  in the interior of his god-self
a second tree springs forth
  and the feminine is born
within the imaginings
  of the mourning god

Abraham and Isaac

The boy climbs
  the rock slope
    gracefully,
  like a young sheep
I feel the heaviness
  of my years
I am winded, tired
  and my legs feel heavy
pained with the load
  I carry

I am aware of
  the sensual pleasure
of my mature hand
  on the hot
tanned bare back
  of the small boy

His heaving chest
  fits easily
in the palms of
  my large rough hands
I feel the small bones
  under his sunbaked
    flesh

I am attracted
  to the innocence
the youth
  the yielding
young flesh
I want to touch life

Yet, in my mind
  I hold the bloody knife

I feel the cold steel
  against my thigh
promising death

His trusting eyes
  look up
to meet my
  hard gaze
obedient
  in his tender life
even to the jaws
  of death

And the booming
  voice
of the harsh god
  urges me on

Saint Sebastian

My eyes always seek him out
  that graceful placid young man
his muscular body pierced
  with sharp arrows

He stops me —
  there is something in his manner
that invokes a sudden and complete arrest
  of consciousness
bringing — a dead halt
  of the forward pitch of my driven life
and an immediate, full and unexpected
  tranquility

The cruel barbarism
  that engendered his wounds and his agony
    is remote
      ignored
    like a disturbing insect

Is he oblivious to the pain?
Or is his a look of gratitude
  to be chosen
  to be so wounded?

His erotic body is fully charged
  alive . . . beating . . . pulsing
    loins sinews and soul

A celebration of the flesh:
  he is the sacrificial lamb

He revels in the sheer erotic delight
  at being a feast for his Lord

It is the deep steady benign gaze
of his clear eyes that pierces me
His total surrender is
like an arrow
I feel the sharp point enter my flesh

Impaled by the totality of his calm
touched by his acceptance
I am penetrated again and again
new blood flows from my wounds

A deep river of warmth and compassion runs
sweeps me away
into an inner whirlpool
of peace and surrender

Tiny Angel

The little girl angel
*   her hair being combed*
*   looks sensuously off*
*   into the delight*
*   of other worlds*
*   and yields*
*   to dreamy pleasures*

Her tiny feather wings
*   just newly sprouted*
peek above the blades
*   of her little shoulders*
stirring tender feelings
*   within me*

Her innocence
*   cuts deeply*
*   into my haunted imagination*

Crucifixion:
*   I feel nails enter my flesh*
*   and a lance pierce my side*

I bleed freely

I feel my heart bruised
*   my spirit burned by the clarity*
*   of the tender image*

Then resurrection:

With the sudden gust
*   of fresh spring wind*

*   it is morning,*
*   and*

I walk in dewy grass
*   singing a carefree song*

Leda And The Swan

Leda:
Your eyes enchant me —
   radiant and fiery
Your soft breasts are
   hard-tipped and alert
Sensuous hair cascades
      down the long smooth arch
         of your back
      to whisper between
         the secret folds
            at the joining of
               your milky thighs

Swan:
You are all motion and grace —
   movement in soft white undulations
The glory of your plumed wings
   stretches out in ecstatic wildness
Your neck serpentine
   yet exquisitely soft
      with an inner vortex
         of tension

The downy arch
   of the swan's neck
      echoes
the graceful softcurves of
   the girl's sensuous flesh

The lush roundness
   of her body
      resonates with
      the feathered fullness
of the swan

Intertwining:
   white swan neck nestled
      within
   tender yielding breasts

The menacing beaked creature
   matches
      the intensity
         of the passion
      glowing in the heat
   of her humid loins

And oh! the joining!
   a dazzle of
      feathers and luminescent flesh
   swirl of
      golden hair and snowy wings
   bite of
      sharp beak on erect nipple

He plunges
   into her

and in the joining
   both are torn apart
      by the vastness
         of their difference

White glory thrusting
   into the sap
      of the ripe fruit

Exploding
   into
      New Being

SO IT IS IN SPIRITUALITY

The brutish nature of humankind is trapped in the struggle for survival. But when one's eyes shift to the heavens and are filled with the sense of wonder and awe, there is an inner stirring of a quest for the *meaning* of existence.

This occurred early in Jock's life. Though earlier motivated by his craving for *power*, his yearnings were always accompanied by his wonder over *beauty, sensuality* and *communion.* These came to be his primary motivators later in his life.

When I first met him, Jock wanted to be perfect. In order to achieve that end, he would stop at nothing, spare no expense, expend limitless time and effort. Like many others of his generation, he became spiritually ambitious, willing to follow any guru, to devote his energies towards any spiritual practice that would offer him solutions. In rapid succession, he became a yoga junkie, then a meditation obsessor, and then a t'ai chi compulsor, to name a few. While studying the Kabbala and the Tarot, he was confronted with the dilemma of "The Hanged Man," the subject of one of his poems.

While wrestling in the inner spaces of his world through psychic means, Jock was haunted by an indefinite image of an exotic Persian figure that kept re-appearing in his dreams; this he attempted to capture in a series of poems. All of his spiritual practices were ultimately dropped when he finally concluded that there was nothing to achieve; that perfection was HERE and NOW! All that was important was to become *aware* of these patterns around which meaning was constructed. Like lasers intersecting to form holographic patterns and revealing new dimensions, the relationship that he and I were crafting served to illuminate our own individual selves and meanings.

Suddenly, it struck us both that what we were discovering about ourselves *in relationship* was a reflection of the nature and inter-relatedness of all things! To know the universe, we had only to know ourselves and our connectedness. Isomorphically, the pattern of one is identical to the pattern of the other, in higher or lower states of resolution. **We indeed are one!**

The concept of *isomorphism* as contained in the philosophy of *structuralism* stimulated us to throw ourselves even more completely into the laboratory of our relationship. What Jock learned about himself matched my own discoveries; the difference is that he was able to document his experiences in poetry.

Because of his love of the spoken word, he even would sometimes revert to writing in Spanish (which he agrees with Thomas Merton is the most fitting language for prayer and talk about God), as in two of the following poems, "Palabras" and "Vida Nueva," which are accompanied by their English translations ("Words" and "New Life").

Finally, Jock has come to know the desirability of *revelation*, the strength in *vulnerability*, the necessity of *faith*, the ecstasy of *surrender*, in living a full life.

Jock's genius in expressing himself in such moving ways deserves to be shared so that others may appreciate and learn. This is the *raison d'etre* for this volume of verse. I can think of no better.

Ben

Palabras (Words)

Quiero hallar las palabras de Dios
Conozco el sentimiento
   en las sombras de la muerte

Pero, no puedo decir o escribir precisamente

Existe un color misterioso
No tiene formas

Tengo miedo
Tengo calor
Tengo un movimiento turbulento
   en mi corazón

Quiero entender las palabras de Dios
Pero no puedo hallar las respuestas
No se nada

Además — veo el movimiento del ave
   y los colores del día nuevo
   y oigo la música verde de los árboles y el cielo

Dios está aquí
Entre nosotros

Tiene el semblante
   de los árboles y los planos vastos

Quiero oír la voz de Dios
Pero no puedo discernir las palabras
Puedo escuchar solamente el silencio rugiente

Words (Palabras)

I wish to uncover the words of God
I know the feelings
   that lurk in the shadows of the dead

Yet, I cannot speak or write with precision

There is a haunting colour
without any distinct form

I am afraid
and I am on fire
I feel a turbulent movement in my breast

I wish to find the words of God
But I cannot discover proper responses
I don't know anything

Nevertheless, I witness the circling motion
   of a bird
and the colours of the new dawn
and hear the green music of the trees and sky

God is here
among us

He has the face
   of trees and vast plains

I yearn to hear God's voice
And yet I cannot discern any words at all
I only hear the roaring silence

Vida Nueva (New Life)

Quiero oír las voces de los muertos
Quiero tocar los rostros de mis amigos
que han pasado
Ahora, vuelven de la tumba
cerca de la vida nueva.

Esta es la vida nueva
sin desesperación
Con tristeza — por cierto
pero asimismo con felicidad
profunda

Entiendo la voz espiritual en el viento
Bebo el agua pura de las estrellas

Este es un país sin frontera
Una campiña sin distinciónes
No son fenómenos materiales
Aquí están los espacios del espíritu

Los árboles invisibles tiemblan
con el viento del alma

New Life (Vida Nueva)

I yearn to hear voices of dead people
and crave to touch the faces of friends
who have passed through death's door
At this moment, they are returning
from the tomb to witness new life.

This is the new life:
No longer one of despair
It has a strong measure of sadness, true
But it is also laced with profound joy

I hear a voice
whispering to me in the wind
I drink the pure water of the stars

This is
a country without borders,
a region without designations.
Strangely, these are not physical occurrences —
This landscape is of the spirit.

Invisible trees tremble
in the breezes
that blow
through my soul

Wellspring

Beneath the impersonal
hustle of
daily life

runs
a quiet
subterranean stream

A wellspring
that trickles
into the occasional
moment

Dance

fluid articulated power

subtle movement of limbs

brings

grace

beauty

depth
into
dialogue:

the formation

of

substantial reality

from the stillness

The Hanged Man

Whirling   wind   cries
slow nauseating torsion
sinews strain as body twists
mind reels as the panorama inverts
vision stretched then ripped
by kaleidoscopic mutant images
before the blindness sets in

Light of day is fading
Man-that-was is dying
Night globe is rising

Stark against the sky of the dying light
the tree-of-the-soil stands
withered and dry
bark stripped bare
leafless twigs its skeletal remains
To the outward eye — a death

The howling windcry fades
into a weeping
diminishing to whispers
and trails off
into silence

Strange inversion:
All that was, is not

Memory grows dim, as throb impels

Silence pulses:
ground for new music
Vision in blackness is keen

Beginnings:
  Roots   reach . . . up
    take hold . . . in flame
  Molten sap flows . . . down
    through enervated sinews

The celestial tree is birthed
  manifesting the one-to-become

Rebirth

Open your hand

   and

    burst

     into

      flame

Freedom

vastness

  surrounds

   the empty moments

I am alone
floating
  like a rootless flower
   in deep inner space

Dream Image

Blue velvet darkness
    surrounds   envelops
    comforts
      mystifies
        terrifies
          intrigues

includes

Light sparkles in darkness
  like stardust scattered

Exotic oasis
  camel smell
  cool sand
    palmtree wind
      strange eerie music

Behind the tent-flap:
  sorcerer's mysteries
    crystal ball   arcane symbols

Peeking in,
  childmind is flooded with
    misted images
      anticipating the life to come

impregnation
  of mind
    with seeds from
      the dark silence
        of
          the beyond

Revisit

In my boyhood, I had a recurring dream:

In a desert oasis, I lifted a tent flap
  and saw with child's wonder
the back of a hooded and robed figure
  looking into a crystal ball.

Now, leaving the moody dream field of boyhood
  I return to the image
with investigative adult eyes
  I lift the flap again
and slip into the tent

From within my hood,
  peering into the crystal myself
I am amazed to see
  staring back at me
the face of a woman!

Overhead
  the moon shines calmly on

Night Visitor

Asleep in the darkened room

A sudden sound
  shocks me to sudden awakening
Heart pounding
  startled
  by a beating rhythm
disturbing the silence

A furious flapping —
  the sound that wind makes in a flag
    or pinions thrashing still air

Something brushes my hand
I lie motionless in dread

A shudder of horror
  shivers through my alarmed body

I sense the soft press of feathers
  against my cheek

Opening my terrified eyes,
  I look into
    the face of
      an angel

His eyes are soft
  the taut muscular body
    strangely cloaked
  in the massive
feathered wings

A pale orange light
  illuminates the room

Prayer

I have not prayed often
since I was a child
But now, I am nearing
a quiet desperation

The God I once invoked
was distant, ancient and stern
far beyond the reach of
my childish yearnings

Now, I pray
to a god of passion
life thrust
imagination
inspiration

I summon you!

Rise to birth within me

heat my blood
torment my limbs
inflame my interior
with molten eruptions

So that I may break free
and dance across the sky

Invocation

O Lord God
  whose form and shape
  I do not know
Be near to me
  and have mercy

Mother of God
  I rejoice
    in your sunshine
  and bless you
    for your rain

Son of God
  I resist you as
  a temptation

Bride of Darkness
  you are the
    unseen mystery

Holy Child
  lamb of peace
I feel your breath
  in the misty breezes
    of dawn

Suzhou Evening

Here we are
  at the outpost
    the farthest we have come
      from our known civilization

huddled together
  in a cold dark room
the radio playing
  a mournful violin
    in oriental tones

I am face to face
  with my obsession
for conquest
  a lone white man
amidst gentle yellow people

Slowly the thought dawns:
  the thrust to dominate women is
an attempt to conquer
  my own feminine nature

Yield!

A warm flood
  of acceptance
    and surrender
  sweeps through me

God is near me

She has
  a feminine face
    and presence

Holy Mother
  Blessed Sister
Have mercy upon me

The Dream

Indeed
*   it is always*
whispering

but now,
*   in the pine forest*
in mid-afternoon

I pause

*   to listen*

Renewal

What is called for
*   is not*
a savage amputation
*   of your previous existence*

No harsh excoriation
*   no cut*
no evisceration

*   No —*

The dawn of your
*   new life*
is gentle
*   surrender*

The sun rises
*   in the opening*
*   of your hand*

Resurrection

I have passed
through the valley
of the shadows

and stand naked
before the altar
of the flesh

In this place of
quiet stillness
there are no images
only feelings and pure sensations

torchlight glows red
casting warm light
into the quiet scene

Reborn, vital
I surrender
to the river currents
of my soul

The fire beckons

I feel a dizzy freedom
as I stand humbly
stripped bare
free
in the cathedral of
the inner flame

Gentle breezes open
the new flower
a delicate scent lingers
as fine smoke drifts upwards

Here, there are echoes only

of the previous pain and power
the torments and compulsions
that were the challenges of the outer chambers

On the altar
is a mirror
in it, I see reflected
my own face
shining in innocence

Reborn
boyhood emerges
in my fresh body

Listen

Rest in the sombre shadows

The quiet inner voice
has been talking to you all your life

Now you begin to listen
and the world opens

Flooding with images
from behind the dam
of social propriety

Accompanied by strange and haunting melodies

Drawing of St. Theresa of Avila by Russell Davidson.

The Ecstasy of Saint Theresa

"The pain was so sharp that I cried aloud but
at the same time I experienced such delight
that I wished it would last forever."
                              — St. Theresa of Avila

I knew I had to see her
    but I was unprepared
for the magnitude
    of the greatness in Bernini's sculpture

The dim late afternoon church:
Scarcely anyone but the two of us
    to view this timeless
        work of art in marble

Even in the faint light
    the atmosphere of the cathedral
        is warm and inviting
    peaceful
and incredibly still

And here, to one side
    for perpetuity
        she reclines
    her divine face arched back
in ecstasy
    her gentle form breathing
        in the milky marble

Such grace and delicacy
    her face transformed
        her body yielding

Surrender:
    every limb and joint electric
        with the imminence
    of her lover

The marble is cool and smooth
a perfect medium to
capture and fix
such a precious moment

Yet, she appears to be breathing!
she is not imprisoned
not frozen — she has escaped:

The piercing of the arrow
made an incision
in time
and she slipped through
into liberation

In the suddenness of the rapture:
she has sprung into full bloom
in the flash point
between times
radiant now — in the freedom
between confining moments

By her wounding
she has been catapulted
out of time
into the timelessness
of cool marble

glowing, shining
in the shadows
of the dark church

Her face emits an aura
that has struck me fully
in the moist recesses of my heart
and in the deep wordless place

My inward river overflows its banks
and I cry out
for wounds of my own